GOD BOX

POEMS

MARK FLECKENSTEIN

Clare Songbirds Publishing House Poetry Series
ISBN 978-1-947653-36-8
Clare Songbirds Publishing House
God Box © 2019 Mark Fleckenstein
All Rights Reserved. Clare Songbirds Publishing House retains right to reprint.
Permission to reprint individual poems must be obtained from the author who owns the copyright.

Printed in the United States of America
FIRST EDITION

Library of Congress Control Number: 2018965682

Clare Songbirds Publishing House Mission Statement:
Clare Songbirds Publishing House was established to provide a print forum for the creation of limited edition, fine art from poets and writers, both established and emerging. We strive to reignite and continue a tradition of quality, accessible literary arts to the national and international community of writers, and readers. Chapbook manuscripts are carefully chosen for their ability to propel the expansion of art and ideas in literary form. We provide an accessible way to promote the art of words in order to resonate with, and impact, readers not yet familiar with the siren song of poets and writers. Clare Songbirds Publishing House espouses a singular cultural development where poetry creates community and becomes commonplace in public places.

140 Cottage Street
Auburn, New York 13021
www.ClareSongbirdspub.com

CONTENTS

PREHISTORY

Postcard	11
Ritual	12
Morning Light	13
Homecoming	14
Flight	15
Nearing 40, June 1995	16
Untaken Roadside Photograph	17
Crepuscular	18
Self Portrait: Vespers	19
In The Dark, Near Winter	20
Awakened	21
Meditation for a New Year	22
Still Life With Ruins	23
Getting Here From There	24
History	25
Love Poem	26
Postcard To Banff	27
Photograph	28
Line Drawing	29
Etching	30
Landscape	31
Portrait	32
Domestic	33
Mock Translation From The German	34
Dance	35
What We Practice in Our Sleep	36
Letter to High School Friends	37
Terrace Songs – Munich – October 2006	38

GOD BOX

First Light In The Worlds God Never Finished	43
Erasure	44
Childhood	45
Conversation With Borges	46
A Blanket For Your Thoughts	47
A Brief Letter To An Imagined Friend	48
Life Or Art	49

Family Dialogue	50
July 1999	51
Misconceptions About The End Of The World	52
God Box	53
Snapshot	54
The Names Of The Stars	55

For Zeynep

Grateful acknowledgement to the editors of the following publications where some of these poems, often very different versions, first appeared:

Sticks: "Ritual", "Morning Light", "Love Poem" (under the title, "Ritual: Love Poem") and "Crepuscular" (under the title, "Three Crepuscular Rituals")

White Whale Review: "Etching"

I Am I, Drowning Knee Deep (A **Sticks** online chapbook): "What We Practice In Our Sleep", "Mock Translation From The German", and "God Box" (under the title, "Gift Box")

I wish to thank the Massachusetts Arts Lottery Council whose financial support enabled me to complete some of these poems.

Special thanks to the late Mary Veazey, Karen Bjorkman, Gloria Mindock, Carl Phillips, and the Rhode Island Poetry Settlement whose friendship, encouragement and criticism helped make many of these poems possible.

It is religion that carries language.
The river of language is God.

~Don DeLillo, ***The Names***

PREHISTORY

The world is gone. I must carry you.

~Paul Celan

POSTCARD

Of course, there.
Years between telephones, between
shimmed words unaltered by light.
sewing needles, night-hugged flowers.
listening for morning crows, the first bird to learn how to
sing.

RITUAL

So for another morning, the mirror's burning at both ends.

Your heart's untied, useless:
One more day –

Go ahead, nobody's stopping you.

MORNING LIGHT

Useless as we are, we are.
Morning again: light, God's laughter,

coffee. Clothes making us up,
re-telling and forgetting the same story.

HOMECOMING

Wrists turned to face the wind,
my heart, a helium balloon

about to burst into fire.
My hair already on fire.

What's your idea of happiness?

FLIGHT

The autumnal blood-stars have begun to root
again, to recover the ground they'd lost.

No matter how I aim my prayers, they burn.
Yellow voices blinking smoke.

NEARING 40, JUNE 1995

If this is where I'll awaken
I could make it a bed.

The grammar of sleep isn't dreams
or inaudible light:

it's smaller and smaller words,
expectations like outgrown shoes.

A shadow wetting the mirror.
If years, one, two, many.

UNTAKEN ROADSIDE PHOTOGRAPH

Invisible among the buckthorns and river willows,
her husband and son fish the Yadkin River.

Sparrows thicken in the leftover after-.
noon light. After supper, the moon

will retire among the early stars.
Her husband and the TV snoring.

Rusted together by dreams, her hands
sleep. The child that will end

her life begins to stir.

CREPUSCULAR

First light a dull razor through tap water.

Up again all night sawing the room
into furniture. Tomorrow we become a family.

The way a pair of scissors completes any room.

SELF PORTRAIT: VESPERS

At any rate, I am convinced that He [God] does not play dice.
~Albert Einstein, in a letter to Max Born, 1926

Your silence or quiet boasts a shadow and full moon.
By Wednesday, names falter. Wednesday,

a steady medicinal drip and vein-red sleepy eyes.
Take all the suitcases, rage suits, shirts and matching
neckwear.

Casual, colorful. Traveling 1st class, a seat to yourself
and the others.

IN THE DARK, NEAR WINTER

The room like a bed.
A window against the wind.

Streetlights burn out, on, out,
on and on and on. Snow turns to water

but gray first. Almost audibly,
her foot imitates dice,

taps itself to sleep
while the other awaits the outcome.

Awkward light. The inevitable rowing.

GETTING HERE FROM THERE

Tooth colored, a dutiful yellow cast, dull, flat,
square, the same dimensions

in either direction. Like longing, only visceral,
swallow (when or if) breathing. Dust,

splintered air, wood (articulate and orchestrated)
now breaking and given voice.

Closer and close to what it imagines,
unbreakable, perfectly

and only a wall, as if thinking were possible.

MEDITATION FOR A NEW YEAR

More and more days with fewer
and fewer words. And those

fat as pencils. My advice:
follow God's lead.

The mountains will be back by morning.

AWAKENED

A beacon flailing and begging for stars, not red thoughts, bony white limbed dreams.

And the sky, an unnecessary failure, end-pinned, savagely wrong and hopeful.

Thinking for God, not about.

STILL LIFE WITH RUINS

Light as sacred bones made dust,
stars emulate God's visible rules.

Is this love? The ancients believed
naming an object made it imaginable,

a door leading to another room.
Closed, then like a heart, opening.

HISTORY

If I live long enough, the clouds
will become my prayers.

This one starts with vowels,
your hair tinseled with sleep.

And keeps the world in place
by hiding my prayers until

they ask the right question.
Luck, a shadow shy behind me.

LOVE POEM

I want the heart almost as much
as the breathy space separating each beat.
Your face above that.

Warm, almost Greek light.
A place to hang myself.

POSTCARD TO BANFF

The way my hands talk back
to the darkness isn't romantic;

the language they use will never
seduce your shadow to let unflawed

color spread against its curves.
Where I thought this would end

and where it has, do not match.
One week's gone.

Your photo of a couple kissing
arrived yesterday. Again, this morning,

I mistook sunlight for your voice.

PHOTOGRAPH

Abandoned voices huddle at the windows, hopeful and know
nothing is to come. Night
tucks the moon beneath its wing. What he wishes
fails. He can neither sculpt air, nor resurrect.
Imagine he is happy, a lighthouse.

LINE DRAWING

Looking up through bathtub water the over-,
head light could be the sun, moon
or mistaken lightning. I do not wish
to die just yet. Without my glasses or shoes

or the towel. Adam imagined Eve
transliterates to even, evening,
event, eventual. Sometimes an apple is just
an apple, a serpent, an exaggeration, a worm.

ETCHING

Even the most broken life can be restored to its moments.
                                                    ~Carolyn Forche

After mistaking a nail for a hand, drawing
I love you in red air, caressing the idea
of memory, a named absence   ,
humid gray, flustered. A picture uncompromised
by weather, blunt, or sharpened instruments,

one word, two words, light, a blue wool coat smelling
of wind and winter trees. Two legs, also wooden,
starch pearl gray, luminescent, bent over sideways,
shoes tired and untied.
Draw breath – as if a hand understands what it moves,
means.

LANDSCAPE

Afternoon sleep smell. Blue, bleached, unemotional, softly, unable. Scared arms, legs, fence-like. Scar-headed wheat-colored hair. One thought interrupts another. Late sun striptease., Curtains, glass. Glass against scratched glass.

PORTRAIT

You urge me, after so many years of silence, to send you the details about my occupations, about this "wonderful" world in which, you say, I am lucky enough to live and move and have my being. I might answer that I am a man without occupation, and that this world is not in the least wonderful.
~E. M.. Cioran, "Letter To A Faraway Friend"

No rainbow ends the tunnel. Rocks
do not bleed, speak in tongues, accrue ambition,
but sleep hard, water-tight. *What light,*
he thinks, birds swearing clouds, abandoning trees,
flight. My occupation. My state. *Sleep?* Move on.

DOMESTIC

Monday, Tuesday, so on.
Frozen together, fish-like.

This is New England. Streetlights
like music, clear through the windows

and curtains. Then morning, its untied shoes and cars.

Children make a house more round, give
it hips. Light

and furry darkness. Wings
and adventure, musical and muscled.

All rise.

MOCK TRANSLATION FROM THE GERMAN

1.

What a bargain the pennies spent
on the eyes of the dead.

One for the ferryman, one for the fiddler—
another year, another sweaterful.

2.

For you my daughter, these scissors
and a penny to sharpen them.

Beginning today, the world is yours
I'll unruffle your wings and make you fly.

DANCE

Another day washing the streets
and houses away, stripping walls,
dissolving windows. A young
woman begins to see who her
body has become, tries to fit
it into what the mirror com-
mands. Seventeen years blink
by, my half-life as a seer would
imagine, not what she might see,
what will look back, and what.

WHAT WE PRACTICE IN OUR SLEEP

1.

Feet nearer blue than not. Veins
like thawing water.

In another room, the cold sleeps
next to our children who embrace it like a stuffed animal.

Birds still sing no matter what lack of light,
color, or moon. This house.

2.

My love, this is how I remember it:
a letter comes in the mail,

the front door opens
as a car arrives, there's much embracing

and it's a marriage. Names change places,
then it's morning again and time to go to work.

3.

All our words, our thoughts—
Will we have enough for the next life?

What should we aspire for our children?
Have I missed the bus again?

are dusty. Another day crawls into bed with us,
erasing light as it comes.

We sleep like silverware and dream
of our daughters, who are music and fly.

LETTER TO HIGH SCHOOL FRIENDS

Let me explain 20 years:
I have two daughters, an ex-wife, addresses

in seven states, an old picture of me
in my wallet. If I ever meet that guy

I'll invite him out for a beer, a drive in the country
and then shoot him.

I spent a lot of time trying to sleep,
then not to.

I awoke in these shoes, re-knotted
the laces and prayed.

Not because my feet hurt
but so God could find me.

I leave a light on all night in case I awaken.

TERRACE SONGS – MUNICH – OCTOBER 2006

And the world is depicted on brief paper.
~from Anselm Kiefer, text by Massimo Cacciari & Germano Celant

1.

A morning eight miles and several hours above her sleep, lacking an embrace. Black wings, white against green-gray, breeze combed leaves. One window offers what another would and won't: clouds taught to smile, trees unexpected, stretch past how she sleeps.

Break, broken, broked. His pleasure: words, worded, wordly. Breaking them, stripping the veins, receiving blood, the heart. Purifying longing, the soul, the air in between. Armless words in long sleeves. Morning
in a foreign language. He is otherwise an empty suitcase.

A four-room world: Physical, Geographical, Historical, Anatomical. Small hands, Saturn ringed, illuminate simultaneously held worlds: glass, ill-eased passion, 5 languages. She arranges flowers: daisies, a sunflower. Her hair. A red striped scarf, safe as armor, woolen, over shoulders.

The sad accident of moonlight continues
like a lover whose face God tore a mouth. No night is an easy mistake, no full moon simply yellowing weather. Clouds, burnt yellow swallow their linked shadow. His foot, her foot, his foot, her foot, his.

Rain urged from reluctant afternoon clouds.
Distant, taller buildings are clouds, earth-stuck permanent, graying. Church bells describe how distant.
This side of the window: an earnest room, two bodies at rest, singular, untouching, silently visible.

2.

Woolen, glass, fibrous, plastic, browning greens,
smaller and looser shoes, inherited longings.
Like a hand absolved of touch, explanation. Tall lights
and buildings swore against what could be right,
the moon patiently waning toward decision. So evening
settled. Black broke stripes, elegant and by morning,
folded like a closing door.

Also ears. Eyes, throat like an always almost spilling
bowl of water. Too light, too dark. Almost righted,
winged.
Page after page, terse silent light. Softly anxious, wetted.

Sheets tumble away from his sleep, from language,
its dark ruly hair. Rethreading belief as desire, confused,
torn, fabulously so. A mirror broken until better.
Strangeness, naively disguised, refuting landscape,
tertiary colors, linguistic sonics, songs, touch. His own
fantasy like late paper cuttings by Matisse.

3.
A star clouded evening tried to fool
the moon into believing one night is an unbending river
leading somewhere. He awoke drowning in sunlight.
Her voice, an ocean over the phone will name
and rename his day. Maybe that's what she meant.

GOD BOX

There comes a day when you cannot revise
your life. It is a good day.

~Donald Revell, "Privacy"

FIRST LIGHT IN THE WORLDS GOD NEVER FINISHED

Your absence accumulates. Here
in the ghost hours, the body

has its own distraction: muscles
embracing bones, the memory-tracing

a face, imagining your breath in my hair.
Yesterday was the same: worried light

covering the floor, the smell of coffee
almost made. Is this love?

Not your eyes, but what follows them
Into early evening:

not a voice, but its dark skin
and broken wing: not stars

but prayers tangled in autumn trees.
Not the moon's calligraphy,

but a door leading to another room
like a heart, closed then opening.

ERASURE

The first blush:
roughed up by the cold,

stars emulate God's visible rules.
So much happens:

light like ritual-sacred bones made dust,
walls thin enough to be wind.

Not quite a language
but questions a brick might ask.

CHILDHOOD

Wind-smeared and bored, another night taps
the window as it becomes a boy.

Yellow pinpricks, yelling moon,
the picket fence like a waterfall holding it all up.

CONVERSATION WITH BORGES

*An unspeakably melancholy memory: I have sometimes
traveled for nights on end, down corridors and polished
staircases, without coming across a single librarian*
~ Jorge Luis Borges, footnote in the
short story The Library of Babel

Gutturals, diphthongs, masticating. Bread-like.
The sound is almost musical. Night

like a plate. Not yet light, but leaning.
Woolen fog, fistful unruly breathing.

Fistful unruly breathing. One dream like a plate,
then another. *Going far?*

That bowl of language.

A BLANKET FOR YOUR THOUGHTS

The room a mistake with a door and a window.
Enough heat to scrap away winter

and skin. Walls and windows still
talking. Air, a wet sheet all over

me when awakening.
Possibly clothes, possibly morning,

light or dark, anywhere. Not moving but where.

A BRIEF LETTER TO AN IMAGINED FRIEND

Gently speaking, nothing much.
Morning, pill; dinner, pill; dishes, talk, sleep.

If dreams, like sleep: sheet, stiff back,
open window. Maybe a voice, clothes

in lumps, anonymous furniture.
If you were here, it could be you.

Large-handed, furry and able to read in the dark.

LIFE OR ART

The stories are all true and horrid
as fascination. Fear as muscle,

melancholic. Conversations
familiar as bedroom windows.

The sun out, possibly visible,
but not here. *There's no place*

like home, there's no place
like home,

There's no place like home.

FAMILY DIALOGUE

What is my life if not yours?
An eye for an eye, a mirror for a mirror,

wallpaper for your thoughts.
What say you?

Objects on the horizon appear closer than they seem

JULY 1999

Fistlipped late afternoon. The sky, gray,
has turned its back as if to say

You want God? This afternoon,
rain. Those are the predictions.

MISCONCEPTIONS ABOUT THE END OF THE WORLD

Night like a night light. Mistaken,
sobbing and bow-tied.

Are you ready already? Think water, news,
luminous and protracted, then, a long

invisible nothing, and all the voices, purity
erased. A stain like a hammer, one last

trapped memory of the world, and crying over
that mirror, freshly named and broken,

the very last thing to ever happen,
and so easily forgotten.

GOD BOX

Unwrapped. A day like a kitchen table.
Knife-clouds, blue, blue, blue sky as far

as it might be. Nothing to tear eye or hand,
but the Kingdom
of Only-After. Erased children in the weeds.

The front door opening like a windshield butterfly.

SNAPSHOT

Embarrassed light and not wanting
to embrace the moonstruck voice
of someone else's lover,
a high school fight song

stuck in your ear,
like waves rusting against rocks
before giving up,
this is one version.

Another begins with lips
imitating how to kiss might look
and pretending not
wanting to scream.

THE NAMES OF THE STARS

Some know the names of the stars by heart
I recite absences
        ~Nazim Hikmet

The ancients believed naming an object
made it imaginable. Believed snow
was cold smoke that failed to escape
its own weight. Used light and shadows
to explain stasis and motion. Some-
times a name completes space until
it is nothing less than that space.

There is something I wanted to
tell you names how two hands
remember how to touch a face.
When ready to believe in every-
thing, giving up trying to name
the only thing they can't imagine.

NOTES

"Homecoming": the last line is taken from the last line of Jack Myer's poem, "Tribute to Cagney".

"Mock Translation from the German" is for Hannah Fleckenstein.

"Dance" is for Sasha Rey.

"Letter to High School Friends" is for James Walker and James Earnhardt.

"The Names of the Stars" is for Zeynep Beykont.

MARK FLECKENSTEIN was born in Chicago, and grew up in Ohio, Michigan, Connecticut, North Carolina, and New Hampshire. He graduated from University of North Carolina in Charlotte with a B.A. in English, Vermont College of Fine Arts and received an MFA in Writing. He's became very involved in the poetry community in and around Boston, for over 30 years. He was an assistant editor for (BLuR), the Boston Literary Review, founder/coordinator of two bi-weekly poetry reading series in Boston and a workshop leader, He's given poetry readings with famous poets (Charles Simic, Linda Gregg, Mark Doty, Mark Cox and Carl Phillips) and not so famous poets. Six states and dozens of moves later, he settled in Massachusetts. He is also a painter. He has two amazing daughters and a large, eccentric, long-haired black cat named Ariadne.

Other Publications by Mark Fleckenstein:

Making Up the World (Editions Dedicaces) 2018

Lowercase God (Finishing Line Press) forthcoming

Lines by an Imaginary East European Poet
    (Half Mystic Press) forthcoming

Failed Stars (Cervena Barva Press) forthcoming

Memoir as Conversation (Unsolicited Press chapbook)
    May 2019

I Was I, Drowning Knee Deep (Sticks Press) 2007

The Memory of Stars (Sticks Press) 1995